The Best Weaver in the World

A play by Phillip Simpson
Illustrated by Sonny Ramirez

Characters

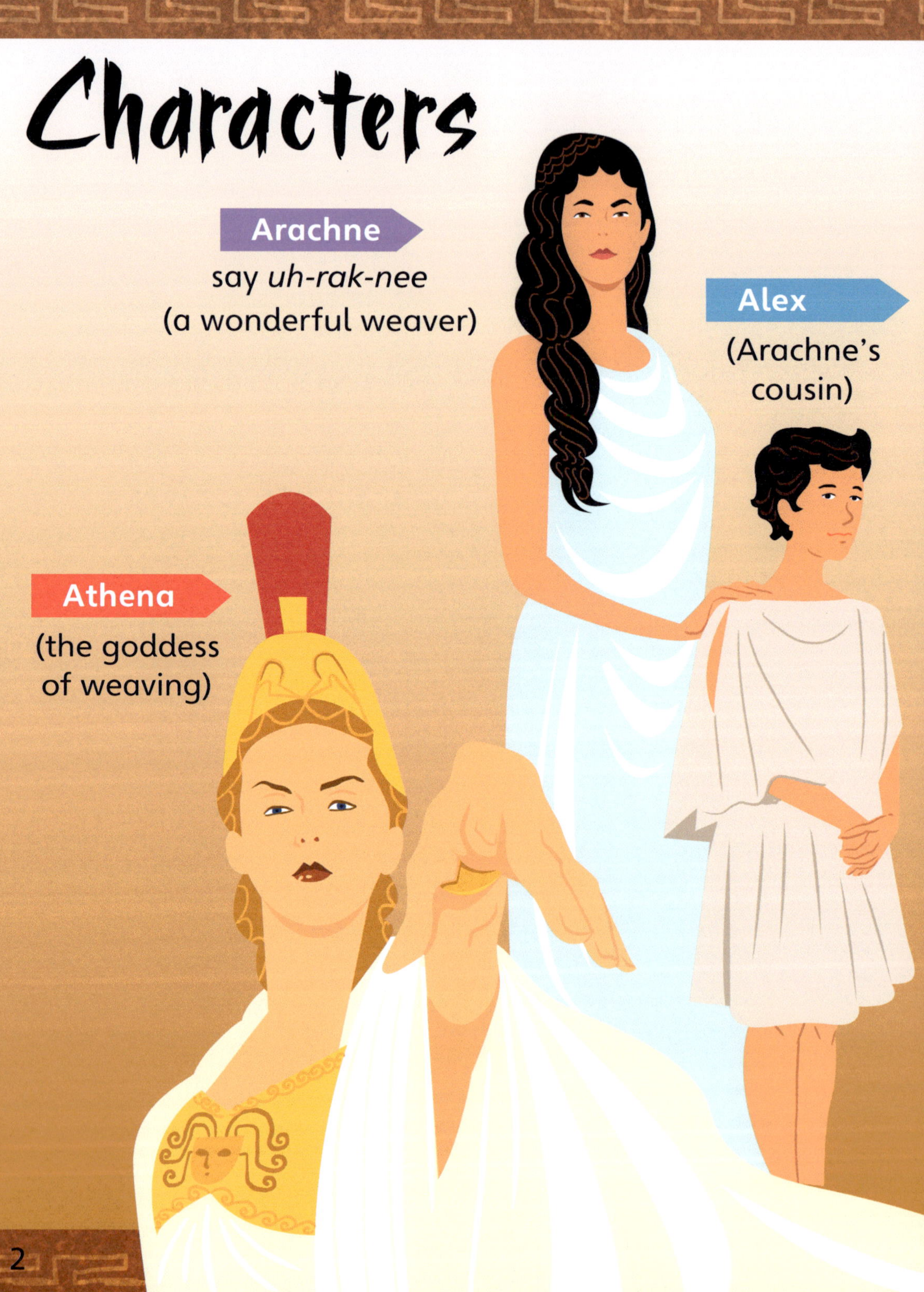

Arachne

say *uh-rak-nee*
(a wonderful weaver)

Alex

(Arachne's cousin)

Athena

(the goddess of weaving)

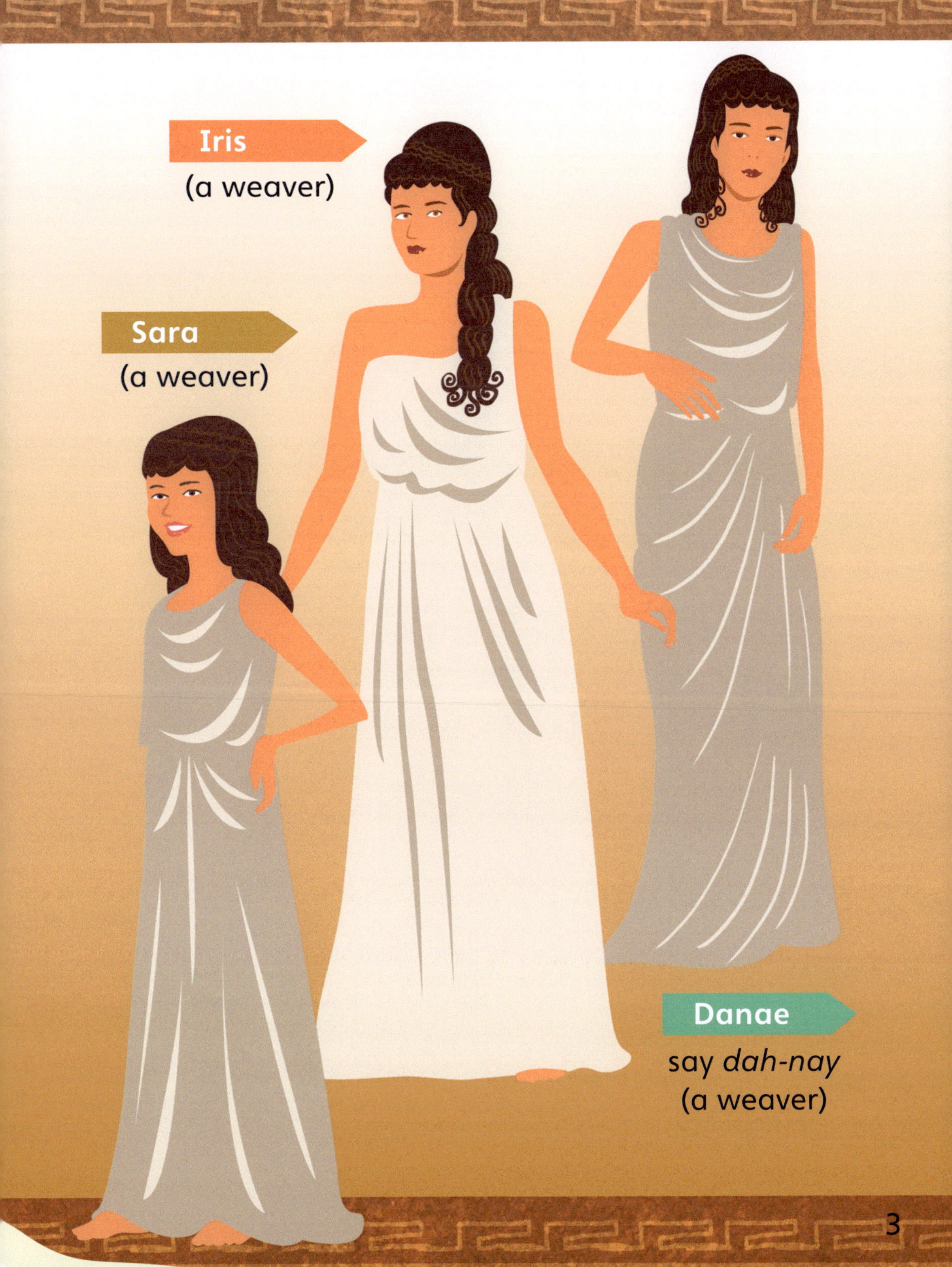
Iris
(a weaver)
Sara
(a weaver)
Danae
say *dah-nay*
(a weaver)

Arachne sits at a loom with Alex beside her. There is a knock on the door.

Arachne: There is someone at the door. Go and see who it is, Alex.

Alex opens the door.

Alex: Hello. Have you come to see Arachne?

Danae: Yes. I am Danae.

Iris: I'm Iris.

Sara: And I'm Sara. We are weavers, just like Arachne.

Danae: We've come to see Arachne's amazing weaving.

Iris: We heard the stories and wanted to see the weaving for ourselves.

Sara: And we want to learn from her.

Alex: Come in. I'm sure she will be happy to show you her work.

Arachne: Hello and welcome. You've come to see my weaving? Would you like to see what I'm working on now?

Arachne shows the visitors her latest weaving.

Sara: Your weaving is beautiful!

Danae: It's wonderful!

Iris: It's the best I've ever seen! It's much better than our own.

Arachne: Well, I **am** the world's best weaver.

Sara: It must have taken a long time!

Alex: Arachne is the quickest weaver I have ever seen. It only took her one day to weave this section.

Arachne: It's true. I'm the fastest and best weaver in the world!

Danae: I can't think of anyone better.

Iris: Did Athena teach you how to weave?

Arachne: Of course not! I taught myself. The goddess of weaving could learn from me!

Alex: Be careful what you say, Arachne! It's not wise to tease the gods.

Athena, goddess of weaving, appears behind Arachne, dressed as an old woman.

Arachne: I don't care. It's true! I am better than the goddess herself. Just look at **my** weaving.

Sara: Ah, Arachne?

Arachne: Athena's weaving is not as beautiful as **mine**! No one's is!

Danae: Arachne ...

Athena: So, **you** think you are as good as the Goddess Athena? You should listen to your cousin, Alex. It is not wise to boast like that.

Arachne turns around and sees Athena.

Alex: Where did you come from, old woman?

Athena: I have my ways. Show me this amazing weaving, then.

Arachne: Of course. (*holds up weaving*) Isn't it the best weaving you have ever seen, old woman?

Athena: Yes, it is lovely, but no one should compare themselves with the gods. Say sorry now or risk their anger.

Arachne: I will do **no** such thing. My weaving is better than that of any god or goddess. I'm even better than Athena, the goddess of weaving herself.

Athena sweeps off her cloak and disguise.

Athena: And here **I** am! You have made me angry, Arachne! You are full of pride. How dare you compare yourself to the gods? You are not better than me. I am Athena, the goddess of weaving!

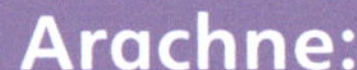

Arachne: If you think you are so skilful, then perhaps we should have a weaving competition! Only then will we find out who is the best.

Alex: Don't say such things, Arachne!

Athena: I accept your challenge. You can't beat me. You are a human and I am a goddess. Who will be the judges?

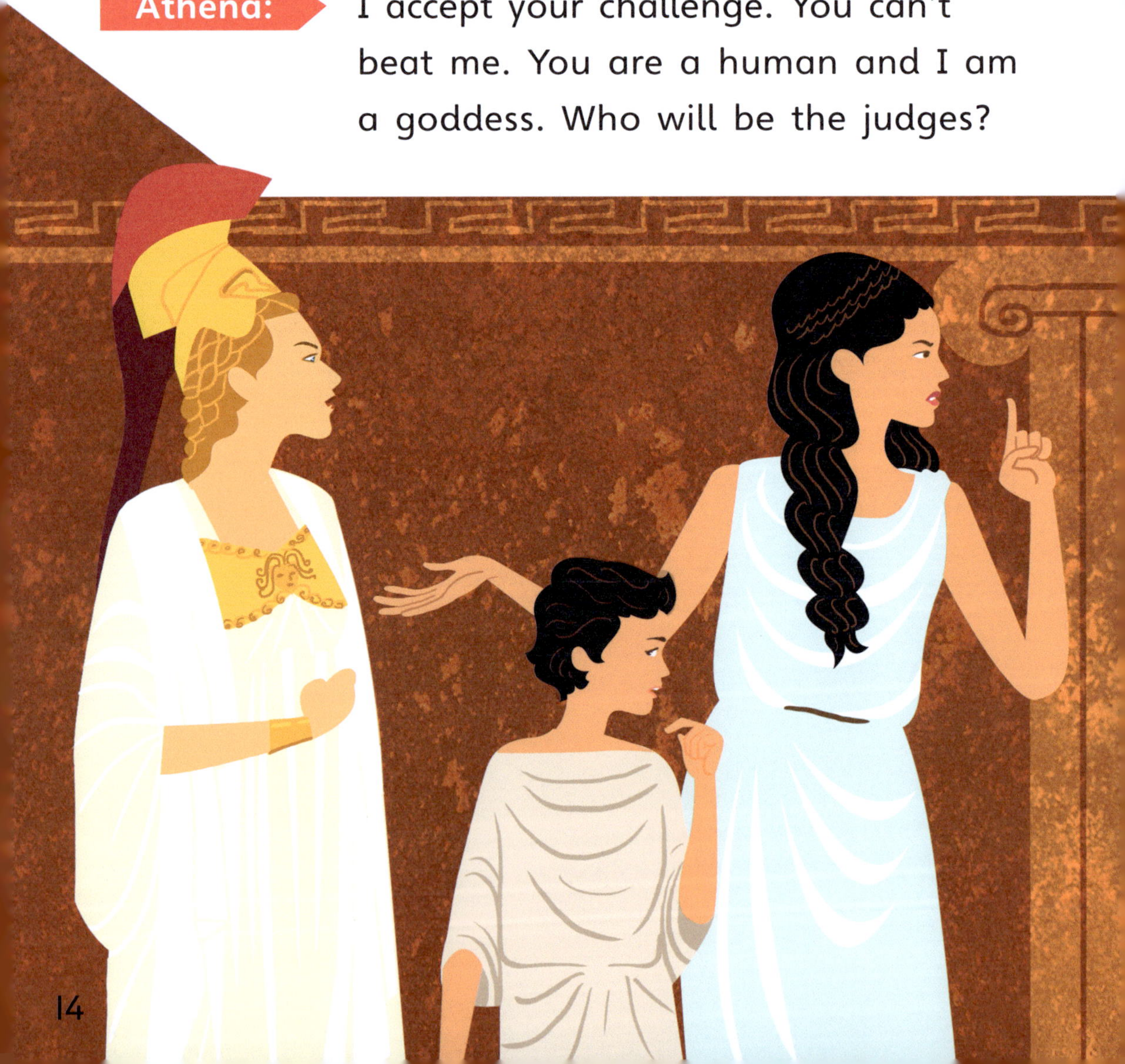

Arachne: Danae, Iris and Sara can be judges. They are weavers like us. They know good weaving when they see it.

Sara: I don't want to judge.

Danae: I'm too busy. I need to go home and wash my hair.

Iris: I just remembered I left a pot on the stove.

Athena: You will be the judges!
I command it!

Iris:
Sara:
Danae: Oh no!

Athena: We **will** have a competition, Arachne, and you will soon see who is the best!

Arachne: Yes, it's **me**!

Alex: Arachne, **please** don't do this!

Athena: Our task is to weave a picture of the gods. Let us begin!

Athena and Arachne start weaving.

Iris: The Goddess Athena must win!

Sara: Yes, I hope so.

Danae: If she doesn't win, Arachne will be in trouble!

Many hours pass.

Athena: I have finished weaving! Look at my work! You can see that I am the best weaver after all.

Iris: Hmmm. Yes. It's very good!

Sara: Lovely! You've done a great job, Athena.

Danae: Very good!

Arachne: I've finished now, too. Come and look.

Iris: It's fantastic! What lovely colours!

Sara: It's amazing! There is so much detail!

Danae: It's incredible! I almost can't believe it!

Alex: (*nervously*) It looks like Arachne is the winner.

Arachne: (*proudly*) I told you so!

Athena: (*stares at Arachne's weaving*) It is very good, but you are too proud, Arachne. People – especially gods – do not like show-offs!

Arachne: I don't care. I'm the best – better than you, the goddess of weaving. I want everyone to know that I've won and I deserve the praise.

Athena: You might have won, but you must be punished for your pride.

Athena grabs Arachne's weaving and tears it up.

Arachne: You can't stop me weaving! I won fair and square. It doesn't matter that you tore this up. I will just make another.

Alex: It is over, Arachne. You can't get the better of a goddess.

Arachne: I can and I will. Just watch me.

Arachne sits back down at her loom and begins to weave again.

Athena: (*angrily*) Don't do this, Arachne. Stop now!

Iris: Listen to the goddess, Arachne!

Sara: You're weaving yourself into all sorts of trouble!

Danae: She just won't stop weaving!

Athena: Very well, Arachne. You won't listen to my warnings. I have no choice. If you want to weave so much, you will weave forever!

Athena sprinkles Arachne's head with a potion, then disappears.

Alex: Where has Athena gone?

Iris: Where has Arachne gone?

Sara: What's that in the corner?

Alex: And what is it making?

Arachne: Athena has turned me into a spider. This is my spider's web and this is how she has punished me for my pride. Athena was right – now I will be forced to weave forever.